AND ANOTHER THING

Patrick Paridee Samuel received an MFA from Columbia College Chicago. He is the author of the chapbook, *A Suite of Heads* (Ghost City Press). Originally from the Midwest, Patrick currently lives in Nashville where he works in university press publishing.

Also by Patrick Paridee Samuel

A Suite of Heads   (Ghost City Press, 2024)

ISBN: 978-1-917617-03-1

Cover designed by Aaron Kent

Edited by Kit Ingram

Typeset by Aaron Kent

Broken Sleep Books Ltd
PO BOX 102
Llandysul
SA44 9BG

CONTENTS

And Another Thing

Patrick Paridee Samuel

Broken Sleep Books

TWO OF SWORDS

So, I picture myself as this ball

of highly explosive material

one of the mutants from my comics might

suppress on purpose to disappear

being a regular thing back home

Nobody calls it brunch

Who has the time? I'm edgy

and need coffee

And speaking of disappearing

Tiffany neglects to invite me

to Fiona touring live for Tidal

inviting instead stiff-armed Lauren

smoking weed in an alcove outside Saint Andrews

It's cool, though

cuz a couple times Jane

takes me out with Cary in her Baretta

Her menthols crisp

how I imagine a slit throat might take you back at first,

resting in the compartment meant for sunglasses

Camping with Cary's family, they tell me they drive drinking,

smoking and get guys to give them these thick gold chains

the racist pigs at our school wear and call ghetto

Generations of our family in the same high school then disappearing

into the lockdown during Detroit's race riot

and the insistence of having to choose as if having a side

as if *HEY PUNK* could replace *excuse me*

No

I think most people don't

know what to "do" with me

Elusive as a shadow, Ellen's husband Jon says

who I smoked weed with, like, twice

I'm fine

except I always feel so pretentious

feeling fruit to see if it's fine

Next month, I'll get serious again

about loving my body

Blindfolded all along

GRATITUDE LIST I

What will I do with silence when I find it?
The taste chews out like gum

Who said that?
An endless well of a handful of moments

You remember all that?
Always was and always will be

Any more surprises?
There is a lake

A lake?
A hand sheathed in silver

Is all this drama necessary?
It offers a pearl

What does the pearl do?
It is offered or offers itself, depends

But why?
Think of an arbor and whether to cross

Must I go?
Your bones yellow like teeth

When will I die?
An endless well

BURY YOUR UMBILICAL CORD

Hopscotch it into the tree trunk hole until it tethers

Until sarcophagi spread from your mom's open lips

Lapping a birth messy with story and spelled to fit a tombstone

Its home an ash for the relic

The twig scab echoes no cry from its pickling hone

Wormed with lore the stewing stork thigh coos from its deathbed

No beacon of morning's applause

SHADOW

Take it to tea, they say

Ride the tail and call the drumming god

Honor the sea beneath your tongue

Print the moon from here

The same mark you always leave

Bath of stamens, tossed petals

Suckle for milk

Clutch your chakra

They'll call your nub a tail

A one-on-one suggestion

Nobody said monstrosity

Just verisimilitude

TOE HEAD

Bleach blonde, you first arrived red crackling fireplace, hot
little Scorpio pft! pft! behind chain mail. Wearing that scratchy
duck sweater, put there to pose on the mantle, I come to learn
that you'll run now at any time, ten white flashes. You purr unclogged
by Q-Tip. A jar of antiseptic where the barber keeps
his combs was a blue Head never understood, either:
swiveled between two mirrors, shown the fade
of its backside, asked to nod along.

THE HOUSES ARE MINE

These kids want to beat me up because all my houses

One of them smells like fried fish skins in the garbage too long

Like one of the kid's hands hadn't been washed

The one at the end of the cul-de-sac gets packages

Delivered on its doorstep from Guitar Center

No one home knows how to play

Always with its curtains drawn, this house

Next door lava rocks and spiky bushes for lawn

These kids cut the legs off their jeans and use them to gag me

My eyes water into houses of slow movements

They tie me with jump rope to the trees they tie their swings to

To smush gum in my hair, pour honey on my toes, poke through
      me with sticks

As if I were a wheel with spokes and that sticks could stop me

TERRAIN INSTEAD OF SHORE

Ditch my legs around any old neck

Trying anything tectonic

Say yay high

Yee-haw

Afternoon conservative radio rounds

The usual aspirin wrapped in cheese

Your pet, your pet

Unhooking my part in all this

As if a perch

As if already scaled for dinner

The English helmeted egghead

Fixed to post a western-saddled horn

FIELD TRIP

I am puking all the way

from the circus, but I hate

circuses, so let's call it a carnival

All the way from the tilt-a-whirl

and candy apple chunks

all those fucking cages

Those circles reigned

to some mustache

ridiculous in boots and a top

hat The bravado The elephant

neck a lady's thigh rests against

has what looks like a rope

from my binoculars strapped

around its neck

from next to my chaperone mom

in the bus air blowing

her crimped hair The kid

next to me eats a ham

and cheese sandwich

with Doritos from the bus

I leave to sit next

to my mom hating his breath

and that lady's thighs, I want

the tigers to eat us all

when they come out

Please just jump up here

I think Or I think

I'll jump down from

the second-level balcony

and pretend I'm the pirate

ship from the carnival

Eat us all! I'd beg

and then bow like that

fucking mustache guy

But I puke at carnivals

from The Zipper

The Witching Wheel

and the metal Hurricane

Let's call it an amusement

park, I feel dropped

from high up

I don't puke at all

I kind of float

until the water rides

until something besides

wind pushes me, I'd rather

be swimming anyway

BY MYSELF WITH A STRANGER BEHIND YOU

I know nothing of behave nor body

As if the sun and moon during eclipse

Dressed for the job with holes

In my underwear and socks

I work too often away from this field

Within tighter languages

Titers will always test high

To keep healthy, I drink fizz

Every morning with eggs

Some mornings

I have eggs and regret

A field to me is where it's quiet

And then my dad shoots his shotgun

Shouldering the blowback—

My version of seeing stars secret kissy emojis

Young though acting old

Old though feeling young

Lovelorn, I know nothing

Thankful to know nothing

So that you'd talk to me

If you were here

THERE ARE BONES AROUND MY CAULDRON
BUT THEY DO NOT MEAN MUCH

No one tells me secrets

None cast circles to my breath without a forest

Without a sapling, and the hole wasn't dug

My throat, so many drawers in my chest sliding out

A pinwheel, a tarot deck

The door they said I wouldn't know how to close

FOUR OF CUPS

So, the first time someone calls me cavalier, I run with it

Saying *there's nothing I can do* and am all yawn

For real, I can't really "do" anything

I am sick of people shooting their shit all over the bathroom

The lower road feels higher

My own burnt roof of a mouth

Blah in the ashes

People on HGTV build tiny homes in their paradise

People should talk more about how they afford things

I buy so much weed

I buy sparking water and hate how Caren calls it *fizzy*

Pail or bucket?

Fuck it, how about soda pop?

Never mind about today, against a tree

And then the sidewalk because the tree fails

I smash the fuck out of my earbuds for dying

For the weekend

For matinees

FULL MOON HEADACHE

Maybe the moon's only a portal into other people's bullshit

A spotlight of bullshit and I'm the borrowed star

Me but murkier

Drawing power from the planetary core

The root is a knuckle swollen from too much cracking

Mouths the moon makes suck the snuffed candle smoke

See yourself from outside yourself

Swimming with smoke and the voices of bones

Maybe the moon is water through a net

Coffee left black

You are responsibly bright and dying

All this moving makes you sick

Crying off-camera post-zoom

Maybe the moon isn't wired

Electrostatic right before a sneeze

Everywhere, there are signs

The moon's move to be my bones

WHISKERY IN CUMSHOT

I am no longer territory:
rootstalk helling its hair
      for the god-talker crowns
           crop heads

      circulate my binge-
      state perjury-free

      a toga soiling
      down
           my spine
      is a mountain

      a fist so into itself

           through irritant
      principle of try is platform

      is worry
           a slippery
      muscle when spit

      my body
no longer prediction
kept politic

accurate is stand-off

WE FREAK

prefer we crawl we tail ass
riding baby-stickered bumpers

meeting, mingling the dying art
conversation proves useless ticks, tisks
frisk and fisting we freak
fornicating the ground down

then the cavity cooks
in salts, citrus halves, herbs
still sprigged, chipping China saucers silver-looking
spoons catching chili dog whims,
flings and sling-back thongs, y'all—sex on a stick
steals, deals
on top of deals
clipping coupon queens, sheen
dreams teeming with teen scenes,
lunchroom lines dime bag budgets, bullying
name-calling is all this is,
cat calls calling corners, pulling rank
all willy nilly

we lenses smear chicken shit
kicker on wheels inheriting the world
before it flakes we can't cool
kid it continually, bearing down
the pastime stitched as a sack all chic in black
running the young buck bald, the cocktail hour

songs our future selves note
more vibration than air,
the catch catching, squats
pitch back that stacked crapper

take a look come on all we little hoe bags,
business suits damn the rain, we hair
spun weathervanes, stars anyway but Monday

morning body, weekend bender eye bag
and multivitamin fish oil moisturizer,
wrinkle wear we fag and wise
women demon breed, all we
high five now go ahead
as if
your neighbor's never been

THE EMPRESS, REVERSED

So, now that I'm here, I'm not quite sure how to stand

If it's ok to let limp my wrists

Tea time my fingers

I've tried writing forever about boys calling me girl

Correct the instructions to fit the copy

I am not mentioned

My mother's coworkers in the back of my head

My man over my shoulder

Recently, I called Jane a piece of shit and thought *fuck her kids*

Enough pretending we're closer than we really are

WHEN "STRAIGHT"

I call vaginas all sorts of things

I work at McDonald's

NASCAR's just fine

Steve's Dad's porno stash

Smoking Black 'n Milds

I change my own brake pads

Forget Madonna

Brushing my mom's hair

I barely talk

I talk too much

My wrists and pinky finger and effeminate hip

Excited for the big game

Experiments in hiding my boner

Boxer shorts bunching up

A good lay

Giving goatee game

My east side trash aesthetic smoke and mirrors

Blonde with sun-in

Cruise Gratiot in Jed's Camaro

Best friends with the prom queen

One of the girls

Imagining elaborate fantasies

I roll slippery in the tub

Thoroughly conditioned

Anything to keep my jizz from sticking

I WANNA BE A POP PRINCESS

I wanna thirty-second costume change

I wanna close, personal relationship with my glam squad

I wanna tape pasties to my breasts in case I get crazy

I wanna get crazy

I wanna stiletto and stockings

I wanna paparazzi caravan

I wanna SUV with tinted windows

I wanna umbrella

I wanna manicure

I wanna burn it down

I wanna sell bags or shoes or skin care shit on QVC

I wanna voice that sells

I wanna spotlight

I wanna play my hometown and stay at the ritziest hotel

I wanna go places

I wanna collaborate

I wanna sex symbol

I wanna hit

I wanna masculine side

I wanna grab my crotch

I wanna pay for at least one divorce

I wanna lady-like

I wanna hail a taxi with my bare pussy

I wanna hold a press conference

I wanna titillate

I wanna dead muppet coat

I wanna bodyguard

I wanna trust somebody

I wanna go bowling

I wanna write my own songs

I wanna problem

I wanna get in your ear

I wanna paramedic to pump my stomach

I wanna pull my face back

I wanna pose like a pin-up

I wanna work hard

I wanna write a children's book

I wanna worthy heyday

PLAYING BUFFY

I carry a knife
in my backpack
in the car
with Pop
on our way
to Blockbuster

Because his head
chips the toilet seat
under my foot
Mom should run
but doesn't

I make the porch
a spot to cuss
at the neighbors

Playing mature
to show them
I can handle it
stake or no stake

DRAG ME

Voilà

Poppy Cock

Daisy Esplanade

Meaty Tuck Everlasting

Hershey Squirts

Truly Scrumptious

Miss Fit

Gloria Hole Enchilada

Bloody Valentine

Princess Fetish

Jon Bichon Frise

Mother Darling

Vegan Dynasty

Red Snapper

Gisha Suppers

Fluffy

Mercury Retrograde

Persona

Marzipan Sexton

Your Judy

The Most

Sue Anyway

Lola Skips

Frieda Lunch

Simone Beeswax

Sheila Meal

Temple Gardens

Baby Mama

La Petite

Stocky Channing

Are you there, God? It's Me, Margaret

Negligee

Punk Bitch

Angela Fine

Aunt Bootie

Farrah Corset

Mascara Faucet

Liefy Green

Stiletto

Chiffon Dowry

Lacy Heels

Pedi Cure

James Mallory

Tequila Shots

Spritz Champagne

Mom of Finland

Starry Night

Chitty Titty Bang Bang

Tiddlywinks

Pretty

Persephone

The High Priestess Herself

GRATITUDE LIST II

You open the windows

You are near a lake

You people-watch

You pandemic

You vitamin c serum

You elliptical

You group text

You fatso

You babe

You go all out

You deserve it

You take it

You lush with lime

You pull a card

You mystic

You imposter

You artist

You laughing stock

You stand in line

You pay it forward

You leave a penny

You mechanical pony

You motorize toys

You have them

You have no choice

You mirror

You curse

You open the windows

You are near a lake

EIGHT OF CUPS

So, this fisher on TV shoots at fish from her shitkicker of a boat

Many mosquitoes bite me as I watch through the screen from the porch

I'm sweet

The ivy lattice pops its pods and calls bees

I wish I could suck nectar with the best of them

Look what I do instead:

I don't telekinetically kill anyone

"Emotional conflict" piping hot in a barrel

That's skin you've got right there

YOU NEVER THINK OF THE STUFF THAT'LL GO
IN YOUR POCKETS WHEN TRYING ON PANTS

I watch you empty
and fit what you can
into a tighter leather

It turns out I don't exist
in the places
I initially thought

If my whistling
would find you in a theater
where I'm saving seats

Maybe then I wouldn't
consider grass a stain
or lie about wanting kids

WALKING AROUND A WORM

You'd be dead under my shoe if I weren't so merciful

So grounded so fucking goddamn meditated

Earlier the tails intertwined

Un-knotting their own grease

Root from source, thread through two flats down

Bent as such blooming tethers

A sky the moon dared call flat

A table without feet between stars

Between veins my leg shares with my mother,

Her mother, and her mother's mother

When I hear the blue mistaken for bruises

SIX OF SWORDS

So, I walk into birdsong after days of pulling cups

Weighing emotion against intellect

Regretful transition in the forecast

No other blue like it

But isn't this balance?

I've dived from springboards before into cocky shows of flexibility

Little splash

Slapped my toes looking for entry, only until caving

This is my take-away-my-power-lock-me-in-a-boobytrapped-room-to-slay-a-vampire episode

Once I access the full potential of my mental capacity

(whatever that means)

I'll be able to levitate and look down on the things and people I've left

AND ANOTHER THING

night sweats my night sweats dead disco ball
lawless coffins, bottles, bouncy shoe bottoms
the boys bottom served raw

my mind's itch a spinal lullaby
penicillin filling beef fat filler
from its freezer, beautician fishing
do it yourself solo poles
the dollar bill nose job
I'm rich

lottery hearsay
lobotomized pro-picker of locks and kneecaps
a pubic bones nice tap nice slice the sluice, nice
christ

the abstract facts verify
the fly guy fad, the graphic
subliminal hint, that one bill in your name

Grace Kelly as Georgie Elgin
in The Country Girl: *all I want is my name*
and a decent job
so I can buy sugar for my coffee

limp wrist slack
whiskey
flaccid penis, jesus

this fostering testosterone's grown gravity
the old hard and hold up fight about money
a bottle of booze for when you're good
for your bang bang hockey practice pipes crossing backwards
shoulder-checking stop spray

star-shaped obstacles
an adult video store next door
androgynous wax
spinner, playing surface and circle turntable
disease: a compass or is it a watch playing parts
rings, hearts
a slippery rope, my overnight bag
douche bag bowtie yuppy punk

dope crowding rowdy busboy slang
grease trap t-shirts grip the zygote bumble
butting hot dogs under faucet, paycheck, cologne

a four-cornered picture strip
magnets breaking storyline
a call that you got there, that I'm here, I got here ok

steak, plates, knives
wine
a fine oven, bedbug eruptions
the icebox white pretzel sticks
brick exposure
the ground growl urchin whose ghost whose house guest waits

shank and wet lip bbq
bareback nerve melter curtail the sequined kitten necks
knicker-knock wigwam mama
flush the eye dye
papoose baby bird sugar schmoopy baby
low opal
la-di-dah
nap

rubber glue the big vote sparkles photo shoots
poolside earrings compressing the heads
print pawed-on make-up
made stanky wedged rain boot
spook, a holler, fuck a gut song
leaning hydroplane
a hypochondriac head shed of dreams
our jumpsuit romper overall flu stall

Mackinac lawns built steps in the thing
ear and tongue between
a number's higher numbers, degrees
whatever
billions should be enough
should do
a body against what have you

COLD SORE NOSTALGIA

The right side of my lip mirrors the flare on your left

We wear them like twins our smiles threaten to split

Instead, we remove muscle from our faces

Vision board culture playing dress-up

Enhancing into something else ingested

Barely hacking the narrative

The reaching shadow of boulders from separate hills

It takes a stranger to notice lip-locked brotherhood

More than any scab to pick us our union

JAM I MADE REMAINED ETCHED ON MY SPINE

As if it were jewelry
    In a sandwich bag
        In my pocket off to pawn
Manifestations of sex
    Melded with fantasies
        Of mutation, art
Supporting the upgrowth of a tree
    No one attempts to classify
        It goes around asking
Folks to carve their initials
    Right into its bark
        Going back
Until folks
    Are left carving
        Into the bark already carved

HEAD BUTT

Go on and crack an egg against another egg, hulls shattered
through a wormhole. I draw a supernova, surprised I don't use
all of each crayon. Head comes back bloody, not stars but spores
behind eyes closed too tight. Head tilts so the blood retreats.
I taste red against bedsheet, and feel around for a cavity
with my tongue. I was asked to make a basket from staples
and construction paper to carry an egg. I had an egg
and was asked to draw a face on it, to keep it safe. Mine
had supernovas for eyes.

SHIT VISION

Tossed aside, crumpled
in the corner like a soiled
bathmat are hands, one
shoveling pennies
into the other's palm.
*That must help weigh
them down*, I think.
Their wrists pucker
like how a fish looks
like it's breathing
when you try to free it
from a hook, and I couldn't
be further removed.

PORN PRESCRIPTION

His fingers are Princess Leia on my prostate

Saying *This ground sure feels strange*

I can no longer pee I've peed so much

And consider stealing his industrial-grade lube

By how bad I have to pee

His top-notch entry brings me back

Into his lab coat, her rusty bikini

An entirely other universe

KEYWORD CRUISE

Daddy son

Super chub

Raunchy otter

Sissy sub

Verbal alpha

Snowballing cum-kissing faggot

Tongue worship

Interracial power top

Nipple play foot job

Fat ass bottom eating ass

Big vs. small

Pocket gay

Sucking feet while fucking

Long nipples

Hard nipple tease

Leather fetish

Silver incest secret

Slut sharing

Milk eating

Son swapping

Tickle tied

Redneck anon

Public sex

Multiple partner slapping

Gang bang cum dump

Piss kissing

Leather piss slapping

Puppy play

Bully big guy roughneck

Denim backseat blindfold

Trade shaved head

Latino kissing

Hairy crack

Armpit

Cage play

Chastity slut

Power bottom group share

Gloves

Gag spit

Spit swallowing

Tight hole pushing

Boot licking pervert

Park cruising

Beach scene camp out

Shoes off behind head outdoors

Wax and masks

Soft whispers

Real guys

HULLABALOO

Hatch the lard cap stirrup me in snippets

                       and spread the tarp

Too pig my pucker snout this snot-shaded doomsday

                          Boy how good my hole winks

   half dead, a calf-need coaxing safe word: I'm set

                    Felch my billie holiday miss hot

            heel

              brass valve the hourly arm

          lengths

           New recruit clock my spot straight drudge my

jacket

       Fear dimension

Can't this system

           update be just one thing already

                 my website's flawless tautology

researching T Tauri horoscopic connections meaning

                psyche I'm pooter'd

I've gone and confused concrete for stone

                Table-tray my puzzle corners first

        Cut the wick its smoking hootenanny

           Sing medievally my instruments

SIZE-DIFFERENCE PORN

I am always the bigger
person, the man in my hands
fantasizes himself the father.

Pull a hats bill down
far enough to block the sun.
You can see

the missed opportunity,
flipped feet
dangling nonstop. Our breath

pools in coos, soothing
the monstrosity we imagine
crushing with fucks,

the back of our tongues
we carry each like children
in need once again.

SWOLLEN UNDER TONGUE WHITE BUMPS BENEATH LIP

Dry mouth white bumps

Under lip dry mouth

Swollen under tongue

Dry tongue sleeping

Peeling tongue side of mouth

White bumps scalloped tongue

Red streaks genital warts

Canker sores dry mouth

Bacterial night guard

How to clean a night guard

Fungal infection bacteria

Tongue in dry mouth sticks

Tight under tongue swollen

Tongue tingling lips

Weeks before tingling lips

Cold sores jump spots?

Cancer mouth images

Oral cancer symptoms

Oral tumors white bumps

Thrush dirty night guard

HIV and thrush

Swollen under tongue

Dry mouth

Cracking mouth

Oral cell death

Dry mouth white bumps

WHY NOT?

Because you might die sooner

Why would you?

It isn't safe

I said so

You'll end up hating me

One of us could get hurt

You're in love

It might bite

You think it's playful

It swells around the cut

Nobody else gets a break

Nobody asked you

It's getting late

Tomorrow's an early morning

It's too hot

We're in the south, babe

Someone might see

There's a speed limit

We could get arrested

Because there should be a plot

I don't want to go

There's hills

It's snowing

It's raining

Your snoring, please

This place is a mess

You're not old enough

You're too old

It's inappropriate

The family won't approve

No one cares

You don't have anybody

Somebody's watching

Pink's a girl's color

Boys play around like that

They don't want us to

It's weird

It'll be too crowded

I prefer standing, thanks

What do you think?

I don't know

Your timing is off

I think it's for the best

It's too expensive

You haven't finished dinner

It's crap

I don't want anyone else

You might like them better

I'm scared of disease

I'm scared you'll leave

I'm scared of who I am without you

The shit you watch sucks

TV is a horrible way to start the day

I prefer anonymity

What would people say?

People don't do that

We worry about ourselves

We go first

What do you mean "Why Not?"

We have everything we need

Why would you?

Because it's enough

There's more

You ruin everything

Their momma won't want them back with your hands all over them

Life isn't fair

We must eat

I wish I knew why

I really wish I knew

TWO OF CUPS

So, we're supposed to believe
Kim Cattrall is ancient
Egyptian in *Mannequin*? Blonde
and named Ema (Emmy for
the 80s) and that Andrew McCarthy
is what, hot? Worth a couple
centuries wait? How's that
grammar work? *Prince & Company
who?* asks Illustra's Roxie
and bonehead B.J. Wert.
That helmet-hair's James Spader?
Felix's Rambo from wheelbarrow
to planter? Ownership? Estelle Getty,
her monocle and who she points at?
Switcher? Catchy surname?
That's the way love goes? Down
the chute towards the chipper?
His hand skimming the blade?
Flesh or wood? Pulp or pulp? Where
others can't see? The big climax?
Closed doors? A motorcycle ride?
Stiff knees? Tied down? Blow away?
Coifed hair and shoulder pads? The rave
window displays? Working nights?
Day? Double? Get her alone?
Doesn't work anymore? What now?
Ask Hollywood? More Hollywood?

CONSTRUCTION PAPER HEART

Hot pink halves

And now you try ignoring me

Unfolding at the crease

You have the city

Gum-glued and garbage-clad

I have the lake

Spit-shined in hand-me-downs

Our spread's standstill

Call yourself a man to see how it feels

Blow me off all you want, and I'll love you

Coca-Cola is love

Calling it pop

Cats over dog owners

Pools to beaches

Midwestern cement

I love you just standing there, pumicing your feet

And how you scoop the bugs and leaves out

Pool boy

Peter Pan peanut butter lies

A texture well into adolescence

A legal twinkhood

Burlier JIFs less greasy

I want to beat the shit out of you I love you so much

Ignore you for days eating junk food for dinner

Sleeping so our bodies don't touch, that's love

Schmoopy love

The fridge is empty

You've been gone, and I've loved it

Come home

I'll wash the sheets

Nothing to get embarrassed about

I have insides, too

I love how we both have them

How we manage to take each other there

THINGS MARRIED PEOPLE SAY ARE THE SAME THINGS COUPLES AND SINGLE PEOPLE SAY

I do

Should we?

I will

Yes

Can we?

No

Have a good day

Husband

How was your day?

Wife

Love you

Partner

Bye

A baby

What's for dinner?

Morning

Come to bed

Hi

Give me a kiss

What are you in the mood for?

Good night

What do you want to watch?

Good luck

It's cold

Can I have a bite?

It's ok

I hate you

I'm hot

Do you want a bite?

Look at this

How'd it go?

I can't believe you

I believe in you

Can I get you anything?

I don't feel like cooking

Come here

What are you having?

Don't talk to me

Your parents

Is that what you're wearing?

I don't care

My parents

Get out

Talk to me

I can't

What do you think?

Leave me alone

You look nice

Why?

What did you do?

When are you two getting married?

THE HIEROPHANT

So, I see myself in the throat your collar chokes

believing in god in a way

I can't bring myself to capitalize on

Daddy's little politico leafleting the street in pageantry

but the steel-toed size of your staff, damn

I don't think you're scared to die

My hairline recedes with yours

as you point out the obvious heartthrob—

the type whose lips are good

for lipstick to smudge against

I'd say christening if it weren't for the bones

This kind of weather slobbers on

(what your robes lining must feel)

INTERLOPER

If I liked most people
winter would be lonely.

In a science-fiction
novel salt becomes

scarce from shorter
exposures to light,

complicating inherited
methods of preservation.

Setting the table reminds
me of refolding a map:

on the roof there's tar
and the concrete walkway

below splits as easy
as skin. A nest unthread

by one traceable line
rickety where wedged

where a stranger, the moon
someone

is smacking perch
against the porch beam.

CHILDLESS

The windows open easily

Take back your cupboards

Take back your glass

Smudge-proof surfaces

Clean for days

Free time

Eat what you want

Nobody grows to hate you

Pinches of weed instead of cheeks

Get your friends back

Date night

Sleep-in

Hangover

Mind, body, and soul routines

Redirect energy

You create and destroy nothing

Trade your fibs for lies

The static between trees

Scant railing

Rubber baby buggy bumper goodbyes

Cancel legacy

Be gone hand-me-downs

Epsom free-float kiddie pools

Keep the dad bod

Tell them who you are

Rain has nothing to do with wind

You are the one standing

The mud is between your toes

HEAD SPACE

Make room for Head for Head is all Head heeds. That is so Head
to sound so like my upbringing so late-night and watch pots
the shape of bedroom window glass against streetlight. Head's
astigmatism makes everything heavenly. Halos a game tossed
between poles. God, lighting is everything. Have we learned
nothing? Head thinks and thinks blinking black space into a hole
sucking us all in. Head and me playing Head's pal drill for
honey, the hone queen bleeds like vermouth and olive juice.
Walking home from here might help. My slur's grown
into someone's I remember.

GRATITUDE LIST III

Altar of pearl, of shell and spray flower

Of leather disappearing metals

Silvers and golds

Of wine if heartburn weren't a thing

Roses with myrtle for crowns

Silks of sleep, my lover smells, my altar

My charm there in salt

In incenses tapped from root

Altar, not only let but pull

Offer breath

Altar of Empress, the deck's Venus

Sweet thing

Sweet mirror that tries

Tap water still good for singing

Blooming and there the altar drops

The dumpings drain

The effigy, the honeyed soliloquy pot

Crossed legs in place of kneeling

ACKNOWLEDGEMENTS

Thank you to the editors of the following journals for first publishing earlier versions of the poems in this book:

& Change: Porn Prescription
Animal: A Beast of a Literary Journal: Eight of Cups
Columbia Poetry Review: The Hierophant, Field Trip, Shit Vision, Things Married People Say Are the Same Things Couples And Single People Say
Court Green: Four of Cups, Six of Swords, The Empress Reversed
Gertrude: Hullabaloo
Ghost Proposal: Whiskery in Cumshot
Juked: And Another Thing
LEVELER: Interloper
NOÖ Journal: Terrain Instead of Shore
Poetry: Two of Cups
Prelude: Toe Head
Sip Cup: Shadow
Sporklet: By Myself with a Stranger Behind You, Jam I Made Remained Etched on my Spine
SWING: Construction Paper Heart
Tarpaulin Sky Magazine: Head Butt, The Houses Are Mine
Yes, Poetry: Two of Swords

"Head Butt," "Head Space," and "Toe Head" were previously published as part of a chapbook *A Suite of Heads* (Ghost City Press, 2024).

"There Are Bones Around My Cauldron But They Do Not Mean Much" borrows its title from a line in Natalie Lyalin's poem "Resuscitations" from her book *Blood Makes Me Faint But I Go For It* (Ugly Duckling Presse 2014).

This book benefited from early support from my cohort at Columbia College Chicago. Special thanks to CM Burroughs and David Trinidad.

I am fortunate to have written a handful of these poems in community with Holly Amos, Mairead Case, Dolly Lemke, and Maggie Queeney.

Thank you to Alex Dimitrov and Richard Siken for their advance support and praise.

Thank you to Aaron Kent and Kit Ingram, and the team at Broken Sleep Books.

Thank you to my family: my Pop and brother, aunts and cousins. To my Mom—to paraphrase Anne Sexton to her own mother: while I do not write *for* you, I know that I write *because* of you.

To my angels Shirley, Mark, Jeanette, and Violet.

This book is for Erik.

LAY OUT YOUR UNREST

www.ingramcontent.com/pod-product-compliance
Lightning Source LLC
Chambersburg PA
CBHW030855090426
42737CB00009B/1242